Learn to Sew
Easy Curves

LEISURE ARTS, INC.
Little Rock, Arkansas

EDITORIAL STAFF

Vice President of Editorial:
Susan White Sullivan

Special Projects Director: Susan Frantz Wiles

Director of E-Commerce Services: Mark Hawkins

Creative Art Director: Katherine Laughlin

Technical Editor: Lisa Lancaster

Technical Writer: Jean Lewis

Art Category Manager: Lora Puls

Graphic Artists: Kara Darling,
Becca Snider Tally, and Jessica Bramlett

Prepress Technician: Stephanie Johnson

Contributing Photographer: Mark Mathews

Contributing Photo Stylist: Christy Myers

Manager of E-Commerce: Robert Young

BUSINESS STAFF

President and Chief Executive Officer:
Rick Barton

Vice President of Finance: Fred F. Pruss

Vice President of Sales-Retail Books: Martha Adams

Vice President of Mass Market: Bob Bewighouse

Vice President of Technology and Planning:
Laticia Mull Dittrich

Director of Corporate Planning: Anne Martin

Information Technology Director:
Brian Roden

Controller: Francis Caple

Senior Vice President of Operations: Jim Dittrich

Retail Customer Service Manager:
Stan Raynor

Library of Congress Control Number: 2013933963

ISBN-13: 978-1-4647-0398-0

Table of Contents

DISCOVER
FACED APPLIQUÉS—
THE QUICK AND EASY METHOD FOR FLAWLESS CURVES!

Jen Eskridge shows you how to use faced appliqués to acheive the look of curved quilt seams with your sewing machine. Nine contemporary appliqué designs, from cute mug rugs to colorful quilts, will have you turning curves into works of art!

MEET JEN ESKRIDGE

Designer Jen Eskridge has been quilting and sewing more than half her life. She is a military spouse to a fabulous guy who is currently on active duty in the Air National Guard. While he was in the United States Air Force, Jen had the opportunity to live in five different cities in 10 years, including Daegu, South Korea.

Jen graduated from Louisiana State University in 1998 with an Apparel Design degree. She is the owner/designer at ReannaLily Designs Pattern Company. In October of 2008, she invented and launched the Seamingly Accurate® Seam Guide. Since then, Jen has published numerous patterns and her work has been featured in popular quilting and crafting magazines. She is the author of *Deploy That Fabric*. To learn more about Jen, visit her website and blog at reannalilydesigns.com.

LEARN TO SEW EASY CURVES

> **Fac•ing** (fas' in) n. a piece of fabric sewn on a garment edge (often turned to the wrong side so it is not visible when viewed from the right side) that finishes the edge neatly **(Figs. 1-2).**

Fig. 1

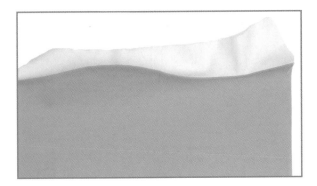

Fig. 2

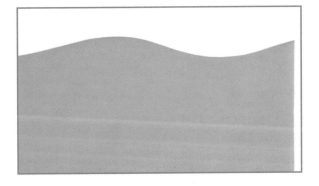

So, what do facings have to do with quilts? Since facings provide such nice edge finishes on garments, why not apply the same technique to the curved edges of appliqués?

Sewing facings to the edges of your fabric pieces allows you to quickly prepare appliqués that have smooth curves and secure seam allowances. Once faced, the appliqués can be stitched onto a background fabric piece or to another faced shape to achieve the look of a curved seam.

GETTING STARTED

To make sewing your project easier and more enjoyable, please read all of **Learn To Sew Easy Curves,** *pages 4-13, before beginning. For general sewing and quilting help, refer to the* **General Instructions,** *pages 53-63.*

CHOOSING FABRICS

Any high-quality, light-weight 100% cotton fabric can be used. Yardage requirements listed for each project are based on 43"/44" wide fabric with a "usable" width of 40" after shrinkage and trimming selvages. Actual usable width will probably vary slightly from fabric to fabric. Our recommended yardage lengths should be adequate for occasional re-squaring of fabric when many cuts are required.

Many of the appliqués use the same fabric for the appliqué and facing (**Fig. 3**). This self-facing ensures that, in the event the facing is not pressed completely to the wrong side it will be less noticeable in the finished quilt.

Fig. 3

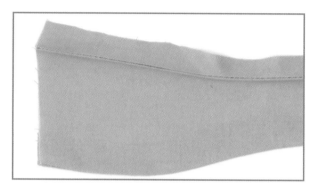

Closed Appliqués, such as circles, pages 41 and 49, or the duck, page 35, can be self-faced or you can use a neutral solid color facing fabric. In **Fig. 4**, notice the "show through" from the dark motifs when an appliqué is self-faced. **Fig. 5** shows how using a solid color facing minimizes the amount of show through.

Fig. 4

Fig. 5

UNDERSTANDING CURVES

The curves along the edges of the appliqués can be shallow, gently rolling (**Fig. 6**); deep, closely spaced (**Fig. 7**); or anywhere in between (**Fig. 8**).

Fig. 6

Fig. 7

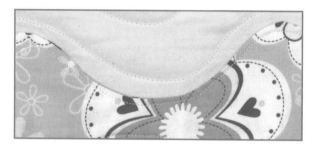

Fig. 8

5

Curves can be somewhat symmetrical (**Fig. 9**) or totally random (**Fig. 10**). They can even be different on opposite sides of the same appliqué (**Fig. 11**).

DRAWING CURVES

The curves in the projects are all drawn free-hand. You can free-hand each curve for a more individual look (**Fig. 12**) or, if you want more uniform curves, draw 1 curve and make a template from your drawing (see **Making And Using Templates**, page 54). Use the template to draw curves on each appliqué (**Fig. 13**).

Fig. 9

Fig. 12

Fig. 10

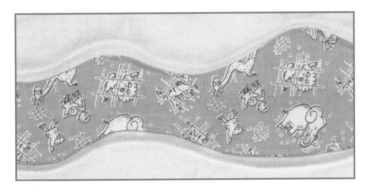

Fig. 13

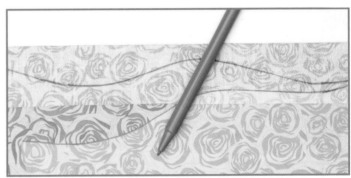

Fig. 11

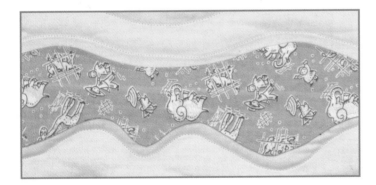

MAKING FACED APPLIQUÉS

*There are four types of faced appliqués: **Single Appliqués**, **Double Appliqués**, **Reverse Appliqués**, and **Closed Appliqués**.*

MAKING SINGLE APPLIQUÉS

Single Appliqués have a faced curve along one edge and the remaining three edges are left raw. During quilt construction, the raw edges are sewn into the seam allowances between blocks or covered by another appliqué or the binding (**Fig. 14**).

Fig. 14

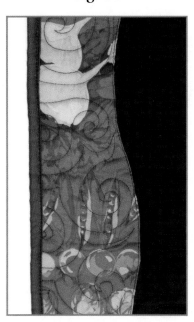

1. Using the **rectangles** called for in the project instructions, match right sides and fold back 1 long edge of 1 rectangle the distance specified in the project instructions; pin (**Fig. 15**).

Fig. 15

2. Making sure the "hills" of the curve are at least $1/4$" from the folded edge, freehand or use a template to draw the desired curve on the facing with a fabric marking pen or pencil (**Fig. 16**).

Fig. 16

3. Straight stitch exactly on the drawn line (**Fig. 17**).

Fig. 17

4. Refer to **Trimming Seam Allowances**, page 12, to grade, clip, and notch the seam allowances (**Fig. 18**).

Fig. 18

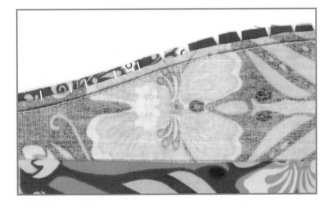

5. Trim the facing 1" from the stitched line (**Fig. 19**) *Note: One inch is the ideal facing width for stability while minimizing bulk, but sometimes because of the depth of a curve or the width of an appliqué, it is not possible to have a full 1" wide facing.*

Fig. 19

6. Turn the facing to the wrong side and follow favoring, page 13, to press the finished edge to complete a **Single Appliqué**.

Single Appliqué

MAKING DOUBLE APPLIQUÉS

Double Appliqués (**Fig. 20**) have faced curves along two opposite edges. During quilt construction, the appliqués are sewn onto the background fabric along the curved edges and the two remaining raw edges are sewn into the seam allowances between blocks or covered by the binding. *Note: Opposite sides of Double Appliqués can, but do not have to be, mirror images of each other. If you choose to make mirror images, you will need to make and use templates (page 54).*

Fig. 20

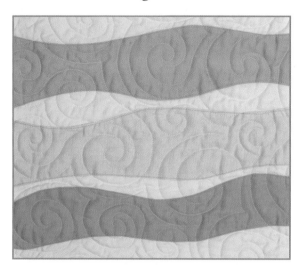

1. Using the **rectangles** called for in your project instructions, follow **Making Single Appliqués**, page 7, to make a faced curve on 1 long edge of 1 rectangle.
2. In the same manner, make a faced curve on the opposite long edge to complete the **Double Appliqué**.

Double Appliqué

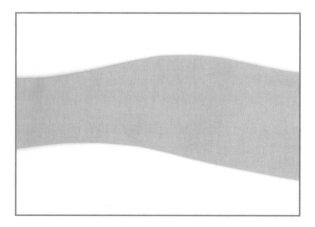

MAKING REVERSE APPLIQUÉS

Reverse Appliqués are formed by sewing a pair of Single Appliqués to opposite sides of a plain fabric or pieced **insert** to "frame" the insert (**Figs. 21-22**). *Note: Pairs of Reverse Appliqués can, but do not have to be, mirror images of each other. If you choose to make mirror images, you will need to make and use templates.*

Fig. 21

Fig. 22

1. Using the **insert** and **appliqués** called for in your project instructions and allowing at least a $1/4$" overlap, position the appliqués over the insert as directed in your project instructions; pin (**Fig. 23**).

Fig. 23

2. Topstitch through all layers close to the faced curves (**Fig. 24**) .

Fig. 24

3. Trim the insert seam allowances even with the 1" facing width (**Fig. 25**) to complete the **Reverse Appliqué**.

Fig. 25

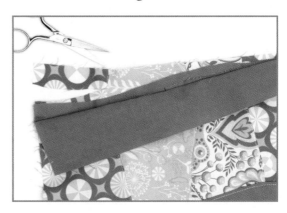

Reverse Appliqué

MAKING CLOSED APPLIQUÉS

The entire outer edge of a Closed Appliqué is faced, as viewed from the wrong side in **Fig. 26**.

Fig. 26

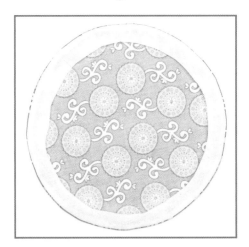

1. Use the **templates** or **patterns**, **appliqué squares/rectangles,** and **facing squares/ rectangles** called for in your project instructions when making Closed Appliqués.
2. Draw around the template or pattern on the wrong side of the facing square/rectangle.
3. Matching right sides and raw edges, pin 1 appliqué square/rectangle and 1 facing square/rectangle together. Stitch exactly on the drawn line (**Fig. 27**).

Fig. 27

TIP: Using a slow stitch speed and a shorter stitch length will make sewing circles and tight curves easier.

4. Make a small snip in the *facing fabric*, 1" from the stitched line. Insert the scissors into the opening; trim facing to 1" (**Fig. 28**).

Fig. 28

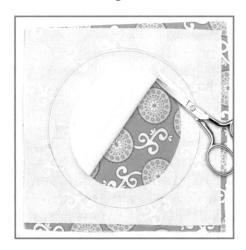

5. For the outer seam allowances, trim around the circle ¹/₄" outside the stitched line. Refer to **Trimming Seam Allowances**, page 12, to grade and notch seam allowances.
6. Turn the facing to the wrong side and follow favoring, page 13, to press the finished edge to complete a **Closed Appliqué**.

Closed Appliqué

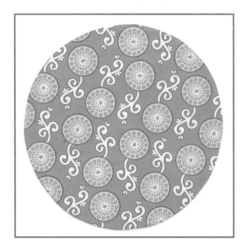

TIP: Want to be resourceful and thrifty? Plan ahead when working on a project with different size circles. Face your larger circles first, then use the circles cut from the center of the trimmed facings as facings for the smaller circles!

TRIMMING SEAM ALLOWANCES

Grading, clipping, notching, and favoring are techniques critical to producing smooth curves without ridges or lumps along the edges of the appliqué and assures the facing fabric will not show on the right side of appliqué.

Grading

Grading is the process of trimming the seam allowances to staggered widths. When graded, seam allowances will lay smooth when an appliqué is turned right side out.

To grade, trim *appliqué fabric* seam allowance to $1/4$" and *facing fabric* seam allowances to $1/8$" (**Fig. 29**). For sharp points, like the duck's beak, page 35, you may need to remove even more seam allowance to produce a crisp shape.

Fig. 29

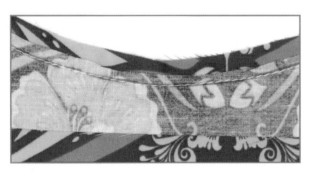

Clipping

Clipping is the process of making small snips in the seam allowances, up to but not through the stitching line (**Fig. 30**). Clips are usually made on concave curves so the seam allowance can spread out once the appliqué is turned right side out .

Fig. 30

Notching

Notching is the process of snipping a small V of fabric out of the seam allowances. The point of the V should be up to but not through the stitching line (**Fig. 31**). Notches are made on convex curves so the seam allowances can fold in on themselves once the appliqué is turned right side out.

Fig. 31

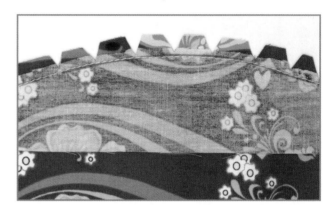

TIPS:
- Deep, closely spaced curves require more frequent clips and/or notches. Shallow, gently rolling curves require fewer clips and/or notches.
- If you have graded, clipped/notched and still have lumps or puckers, check your stitching line. Make sure the line is actually curved and smooth and has no corners or spikes.
- If the stitching line is smooth, turn the shape back to the wrong side and add more clips/notches. In some very tight curves, you may even need to clip or notch every $1/8$".
- If the line is stitched straight and there are ample clips/notches, the problem may be that the clips/notches are not cut close enough to the stitching line.

Favoring

Favoring is the process of pressing an appliqué from the facing side while pulling the facing slightly, allowing a tiny bit of the appliqué fabric to roll to the wrong (facing) side (**Figs. 32-33**). This will ensure that once the appliqué is added to the quilt, none of the facing fabric will be seen.

Fig. 32

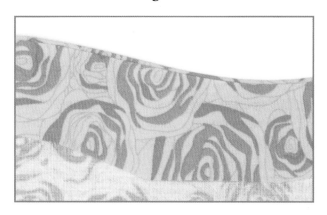

Fig. 33

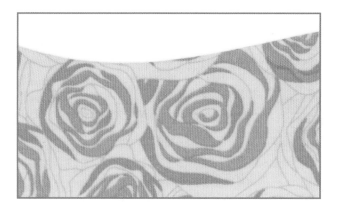

ADDING THE APPLIQUÉS

Pin the finished appliqué to the background square, rectangle, or another appliqué as directed in the project instructions. Using general-purpose thread in a color to match the appliqué fabric, straight stitch about $1/16$"-$1/8$" from the curved edge(s) of the appliqué (**Fig. 34**).

Fig. 34

TIP: To make your stitching a design feature, you may wish to use contrasting thread or even a decorative machine stitch, such as a Blanket Stitch.

WIDE STRIPES

THIS REVERSE APPLIQUÉ QUILT IS A SNAP TO MAKE. THE LARGE INSERTS PROVIDE THE PERFECT PLACE TO SHOWCASE A SPECIAL QUILTING DESIGN. INSTRUCTIONS AND FABRIC REQUIREMENTS FOR ALL VERSIONS ARE BASED ON VERSION 1. VERSIONS 2 AND 3 ARE SHOWN ON PAGE 17.

VERSION 1
Finished Quilt Size: approximately 43" x 61" (109 cm x 155 cm)

WHAT YOU WILL NEED
Yardage is based on 43"/44" (109 cm/112 cm) fabric with a usable width of 40".
- $^1/_2$ yd (46 cm) *each* of 5 assorted orange print fabrics (main fabrics)
- $^1/_2$ yd (46 cm) of dark brown solid fabric (inserts)
- $^1/_2$ yd (46 cm) of light brown solid fabric (inserts)
- $3^7/_8$ yds (3.5 m) of backing fabric
- $^1/_2$ yd (46 cm) of binding fabric
- 51" x 69" (130 cm x 175 cm) rectangle of batting
- Removable fabric marking pen or pencil

CUTTING
Cut all strips across the selvage to selvage width of the fabric. All measurements include $^1/_4$" seam allowances.

From *each* orange print fabric:
- Cut 1 **strip** $12^1/_2$" wide.

From dark brown solid fabric:
- Cut 1 strip $12^1/_2$" wide. From this strip, cut 3 **inserts** $12^1/_2$" x 10".

From light brown solid fabric:
- Cut 1 strip $12^1/_2$" wide. From this strip, cut 2 **inserts** $12^1/_2$" x 10".

From binding fabric:
- Cut 6 **binding strips** $2^1/_2$" wide.

MAKING THE QUILT TOP
Match right sides and raw edges and use a $^1/_4$" seam allowance unless otherwise noted.

1. Lay 1 **strip**, right side up, on work surface. Measuring anywhere between 6"-12" from 1 short edge, make a vertical cut through the strip (**Fig. 1**) to make a pair of **rectangles**. *Note: To off-set the inserts, vary the cutting distance from the short edge of each strip between 6"-12".*

Fig. 1

6"-12"

Continued on page 16.

Wide Stripes continued.

2. Fold each newly cut edge of **rectangles** approximately 2" to the right side; pin (**Fig. 2**). Follow **Making Single Appliqués**, page 7, to make a gently rolling faced curve along each folded edge to make 1 pair of **single appliqués**. Make 5 pairs of single appliqués.

Fig. 2

Single Appliqué (make 5 pairs)

3. Position 1 pair of single appliqués on 1 **insert**. Adjust the appliqué spacing to expose the desired amount of insert fabric. Follow **Making Reverse Appliqués**, page 9, to make a **reverse appliqué**. Make 5 reverse appliqués.

Reverse Appliqué (make 5)

4. Matching long edges, arrange reverse appliqués into **Rows** on a work surface or design wall. Adjust the positions by shifting reverse appliqués right or left until you have a pleasing arrangement (**Fig. 3**); pin. Sew Rows together.

Fig. 3

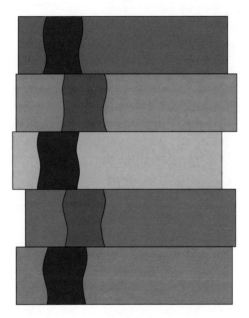

5. Using the shortest Row on each side as a guide, square the side edges (**Fig. 4**) to complete the **Quilt Top**.

Fig. 4

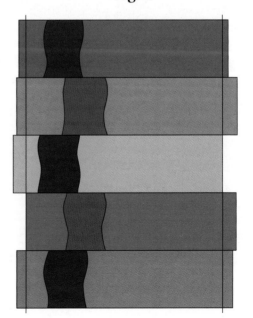

COMPLETING THE QUILT

1. Follow **Quilting**, page 55, to mark, layer, and quilt as desired. The model is machine quilted with a feather design in each insert and a swirl pattern over the remainder of the quilt.
2. If desired, follow **Adding A Hanging Sleeve**, page 59, to make and attach a hanging sleeve.
3. Use **binding strips** and follow **Binding**, page 59, to make and attach **straight-grain binding**.

VERSIONS 2 AND 3

*   For Version 2, the rectangles are cut from 3 assorted blue print fabrics. The inserts are cut from 4 assorted red/blue/white print fabrics.

*   For Version 3, the rectangles are cut from 5 assorted blue or blue/green print fabrics. The owl inserts were pieced using a brown print and a novelty print. The remaining 2 inserts were cut from a brown/white polka dot fabric. The binding is pieced from strips cut from each blue and blue/green fabric.

VARIATIONS

With some simple changes it's easy to alter the size of this quilt.

*   For a longer quilt, make and add additional rows of reverse appliqués.

*   For a slightly wider quilt, cut the inserts wider than 10" or even add a second or third insert to each reverse appliqué.

*   For a very wide quilt, cut 2 strips for each reverse appliqué. Sew 2 strips together along the short edges. Make the vertical cuts for the inserts as far from 1 short edge as desired.

VERSION 2

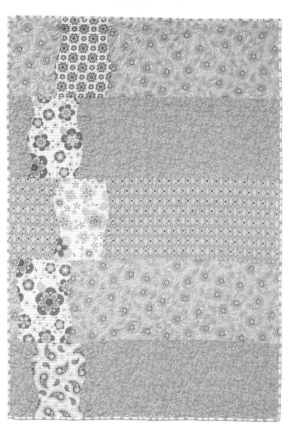

VERSION 3

GENTLE CURVES

THIS EYE-CATCHING BED-SIZE QUILT FEATURES SINGLE APPLIQUÉS
SEWN TOGETHER TO MAKE STRIP SETS. THE STRIP SETS ARE CUT INTO SMALLER
PIECES AND USED FOR BLOCK INSERTS. IT'S FAST, FUN, AND EASY!

Finished Quilt Size: 76" x 91" (193 cm x 231 cm)
Finished Block Size: 15" x 15" (38 cm x 38 cm)

WHAT YOU WILL NEED

*Yardage is based on 43"/44" (109 cm/112 cm) fabric
with a usable width of 40".*

- $7^1/8$ yds (6.5 m) of cream/grey print fabric
  (main fabric)
- $5/8$ yd (57 cm) *each* of 15 assorted print
  fabrics (insert fabric)
- 7 yds (6.4 m) of backing fabric
- $7/8$ yd (80 cm) of binding fabric
- 84" x 99" (213 cm x 251 cm) rectangle
  of batting
- Removable fabric marking pen or pencil

CUTTING

*Cut all strips across the selvage to selvage width of the
fabric. All measurements include $1/4$" seam allowances.*

From cream/grey print fabric:
- Cut 15 strips $15^1/2$" wide. From these
  strips, cut 60 **rectangles** $15^1/2$" x 9".

From assorted print fabrics:
- Cut a *total* of 36 **strips** 6" wide.

From binding fabric:
- Cut 10 **binding strips** $2^1/2$" wide.

MAKING THE QUILT TOP

*Match right sides and raw edges and use a $1/4$" seam
allowance unless otherwise noted.*

Making The Strip Sets

1. Fold 1 long edge of 1 **strip** approximately
   $1^1/2$" to the right side; pin (**Fig. 1**). Following
   Making Single Appliqués, page 7, make
   a shallow, gently rolling faced curve along
   folded edge to make **appliqué A**. Make
   30 appliqué A's. Leave 6 strips unfaced.

Fig. 1

Appliqué A (make 30)

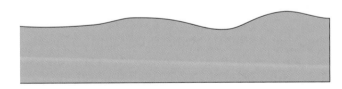

2. For each strip set, select 1 **unfaced strip** and
   5 **appliqué A's** from assorted print fabrics.
   Label the unfaced strip #1 and the appliqué
   A's #2-#6.

Continued on page 20.

Gentle Curves continued.

3. Lay strip #1 right side up on a work surface. Position appliqué A #2 over raw edge of strip #1, making sure appliqué A #2 overlaps the raw edge of strip #1 by at least a $^1/_4$" (**Fig. 2**); pin.

Fig. 2

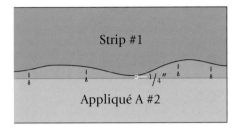

4. Topstitch through all layers close to the faced curve (**Fig. 3**).

Fig. 3

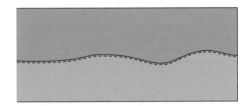

5. In the same manner, position appliqué A #3 over raw edge of appliqué A #2; pin and topstitch (**Fig. 4**).

Fig. 4

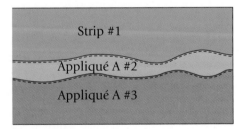

6. Continue adding appliqué A's #4 - #6 to make a strip set measuring at least $16^1/_2$" high. Trim seam allowances. Make 6 **strip sets**.

Strip Set (make 6)

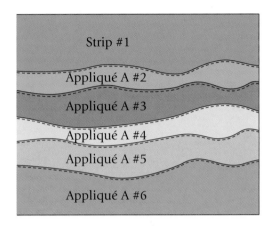

7. Cut across each strip set at 8" intervals to make **pieced inserts**. Make a total of 30 pieced inserts. Trim each pieced insert to 8" x $15^1/_2$".

Pieced Insert (make 30)

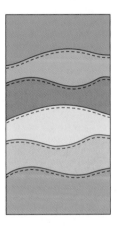

Continued on page 22.

Quilt Top Diagram

MUG RUGS

Mug Rugs are small quilts just the right size to hold a coffee mug and dessert plate. Instructions and fabric requirements for all versions are based on Version 1. Versions 2 and 3 are shown on page 27.

VERSION 1
Finished Mug Rug Size: 11" x 7" (28 cm x 18 cm)

WHAT YOU WILL NEED
Yardage is based on 43"/44" (109 cm/112 cm) fabric with a usable width of 40". Fabric requirements are for 6 Mug Rugs.

$5/8$ yd (57 cm) of grey print fabric (main fabric)
$1/4$ yd (23 cm) of grey solid fabric (leaves)
$1/8$ yd (11 cm) of green solid fabric (inserts)
$7/8$ yd (80 cm) of backing fabric
$5/8$ yd (57 cm) of binding fabric
32" x 30" (81 cm x 76 cm) rectangle of heat-resistant batting such as Insul-Bright® or Insul Fleece™
Template plastic
Black fine-point permanent felt-tip pen
Removable fabric marking pen or pencil

CUTTING THE PIECES
Cut all strips across the selvage to selvage width of the fabric. All measurements include $1/4$" seam allowances. Follow Making And Using Templates, page 54, to use small leaf pattern, page 26.

From grey print fabric:
- Cut 3 strips 6" wide. From these strips, cut 6 **rectangles** 15" x 6".

From grey solid fabric:
- Cut 12 **small leaves**. Cut 12 **small leaves reversed**.

From green solid fabric:
- Cut 1 strip 3" wide. From this strip, cut 6 **inserts** 3" x 6".

From backing fabric:
- Cut 2 strips 14" wide. From these strips, cut 6 **backing rectangles** 14" x 10".

From binding fabric:
- Cut 8 **binding strips** $2^1/2$" wide.

From batting:
- Cut 6 **batting rectangles** 14" x 10".

MAKING THE MUG RUG TOPS
Match right sides and raw edges and use a $1/4$" seam allowance unless otherwise noted.

1. Lay 1 **rectangle**, right side up, on work surface. Measuring anywhere between 4"-8" from 1 short edge, make a vertical cut (**Fig. 1**) to make a pair of **small rectangles**.

Fig. 1

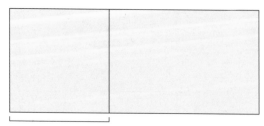

4"-8"

Continued on page 26.

2. Fold each newly cut edge of the small rectangles approximately 2" to the right side; pin (**Fig. 2**). Follow **Making Single Appliqués**, page 7, to make a faced curve along each folded edge to make 1 pair of **appliqués**. Make 6 pairs of appliqués.

Fig. 2

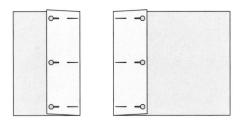

Appliqué (make 6 pairs)

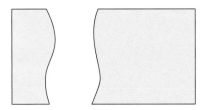

3. Position 1 pair of appliqués on 1 **insert**. Adjust appliqué spacing to expose desired amount of insert fabric. Follow **Making Reverse Appliqués**, page 9, to make a **reverse appliqué**.

4. Trim reverse appliqué to 10" x 6" to make **Mug Rug Top**. Make 6 Mug Rug Tops.

Mug Rug Top (make 6)

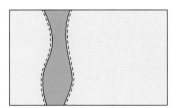

5. For each leaf, match right sides and leave a 2" opening along 1 edge to sew 1 **leaf** and 1 **leaf reversed** together (**Fig. 5**). Refer to **Trimming Seam Allowances**, page 12, to trim seam allowances.

Fig. 5

2"

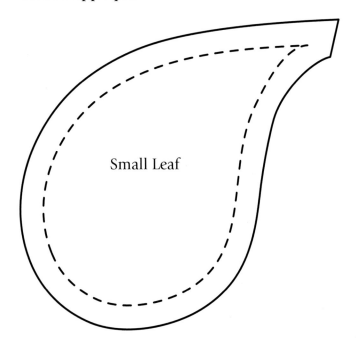

Small Leaf

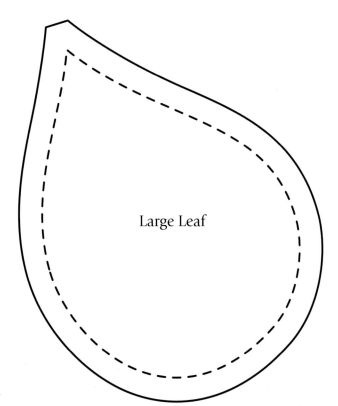

Large Leaf

6. Turn leaf right side out. Fold seam allowances of opening to the inside and hand sew opening closed; press. Make 12 leaves.

Leaf (make 12)

COMPLETING THE MUG RUGS

1. Using Mug Rug Tops, **batting rectangles,** and **backing rectangles,** follow **Quilting,** page 55, to mark, layer, and quilt as desired. The models are machine quilted with an all-over leaf design.

2. Use **binding strips** and follow **Binding,** page 59, to make and attach **straight-grain binding**.

3. Placing as desired, pin 2 leaves to each Mug Rug. Straight stitch through the center of each leaf to make "veins".

VERSIONS 2 AND 3

- For Version 2, cut rectangles 15" x 7" and trim mug rug tops to $10^1/_2$" x $6^1/_2$". Use the large leaf pattern, page 26, to cut 2 leaves and 2 leaves reversed.

- For Version 3, cut rectangles 13" x 6" and trim mug rug tops to $8^1/_2$" x $5^1/_2$". Use the small leaf pattern, page 26, to cut 1 leaf and 1 leaf reversed from 2 coordinating fabrics.

VERSION 2
Finished Size: 11" x 7"

VERSION 3
Finished Size: 9" x 6"

SERENITY I

JUST AS THE NAME IMPLIES, THIS BED-SIZE QUILT WITH ITS CALMING
COLORS AND GENTLE CURVES, WILL ADD A TOUCH OF SERENITY TO ANY BEDROOM.

Finished Quilt Size: 76" x 91" (193 cm x 231 cm)
Finished Block Size: 15" x 15" (38 cm x 38 cm)

WHAT YOU WILL NEED
*Yardage is based on 43"/44" (109 cm/112 cm) fabric
with a usable width of 40".*

2³/₈ yds (2.2 m) *each* of 3 assorted solid
  light-colored fabrics (background)
1¹/₂ yds (1.4 m) *each* of 6 assorted solid
  color fabrics (appliqués)
7 yds (6.4 m) of backing fabric
³/₄ yd (69 cm) of binding fabric
84" x 99" (213 cm x 251 cm) rectangle
  of batting
Removable fabric marking pen or pencil

CUTTING
*Cut all strips across the selvage to selvage width of the
fabric. All measurements include ¹/₄" seam allowances.*
From *each* light-colored fabric:
- Cut 5 strips 15¹/₂" wide. From these strips,
  cut 10 **backgrounds** 15¹/₂" x 15¹/₂".
From *each* assorted fabric:
- Cut 3 strips 15¹/₂" wide. From these strips,
  cut 15 **rectangles** 8" x 15¹/₂".*
From binding fabric:
- Cut 9 **binding strips** 2¹/₂" wide.

* Depending on the usable width of your fabric,
the last rectangle of each strip may be wider than
8"; do not trim. You can use this rectangle as is to
add variety to your appliqué widths.

MAKING THE QUILT TOP
*Match right sides and raw edges and use a ¹/₄" seam
allowance unless otherwise noted.*

1. Fold 1 long edge of 1 **rectangle** approximately
   2" to the right side; pin (**Fig. 1**). Follow
   Making Double Appliqués, page 9, to make
   gently rolling faced curves along *each* long
   edge to make **appliqué**. Make 90 appliqués.

Fig. 1

Appliqué (make 90)

2. On a design wall or large work surface,
   arrange **backgrounds** into 6 rows of
   5 squares each.

Continued on page 30.

3. Allowing at least ¹/₄" for seam allowances on background *sides* and matching raw edges on top and bottom, randomly position 2-3 **appliqués** on each background (**Fig. 2**). *Note: After assembling the rows you will be able to add appliqués to fill in any areas with too much background showing or cover the seams between blocks (the model has a total of 82 appliqués).*

TIP: There is no right or wrong way to arrange your appliqués or backgrounds. You can vary the location and number of appliqués on each background or change the order of the backgrounds—just have fun with it!

Fig. 2

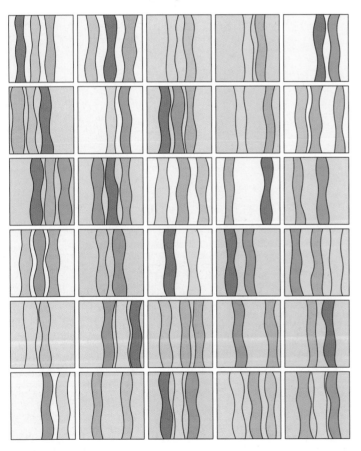

4. When satisfied with the placement, pin appliqués in place. Topstitch close to the faced curves of each appliqué to make **Block**. Make 30 Blocks.

Block (make 30)

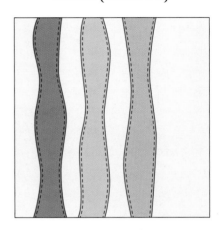

5. Keeping Blocks in the same order as your design wall, sew 5 Blocks together to make a **Row**. Make 6 Rows. If desired, add appliqués to cover seams or fill in any open areas.
6. Sew Rows together to complete **Quilt Top**.

COMPLETING THE QUILT

1. Follow **Quilting**, page 55, to mark, layer, and quilt as desired. The model is machine quilted with an all-over swirl pattern.
2. If desired, follow **Adding A Hanging Sleeve**, page 59, to make and attach a hanging sleeve.
3. Use **binding strips** and follow **Binding**, page 59, to make and attach **straight-grain binding**.

SERENITY 2

THIS HAPPY QUILT IS SURE TO BE A HIT WITH ANY LITTLE (OR BIG)
PRINCESS. BRIGHT PRINTS, HIGH-LOFT BATTING, AND ECHO QUILTING
COMBINE TO MAKE THE APPLIQUÉS REALLY STAND OUT. AND, IT'S JUST
THE RIGHT SIZE FOR A WALL HANGING, CRIB QUILT, OR LAP THROW.

Finished Quilt Size: 46" x 61" (117 cm x 155 cm)
Finished Block Size: 15" x 15" (38 cm x 38 cm)

WHAT YOU WILL NEED
*Yardage is based on 43"/44" (109 cm/112 cm) fabric
with a usable width of 40".*
- 1¹/₂ yds (1.4 m) *each* of 2 light pink solid
  fabrics (background)
- ¹/₂ yd (46 cm) *each* of 8 assorted pink
  print fabrics (appliqués)
- 3⁷/₈ yds (3.5 m) of backing fabric
- ⁵/₈ yd (57 cm) of binding fabric
- 54" x 69" (137 cm x 175 cm) rectangle
  of batting
- Removable fabric marking pen or pencil

CUTTING
*Cut all strips across the selvage to selvage width of the
fabric. All measurements include ¹/₄" seam allowances.*
From *each* light pink solid fabric:
- Cut 3 strips 15¹/₂" wide. From these strips,
  cut 6 **backgrounds** 15¹/₂" x 15¹/₂".

From *each* assorted pink print fabric:
- Cut 2 strips 8" wide. From these strips,
  cut a *total* of 29 **rectangles** 8" x 15¹/₂".

From binding fabric:
- Cut 7 **binding strips** 2¹/₂" wide.

MAKING THE QUILT TOP
*Match right sides and raw edges and use a ¹/₄" seam
allowance unless otherwise noted.*

1. Fold 1 long edge of 1 **rectangle** approximately
   2" to the right side; pin (**Fig. 1**). Follow
   Making Double Appliqués, page 9, to make
   gently rolling faced curves along *each* long
   edge to make **appliqué**. Make 29 appliqués.

Fig. 1

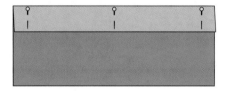

Appliqué (make 29)

2. On a design wall or large work surface,
   arrange the **backgrounds** into 4 rows
   of 3 backgrounds each.

Continued on page 34.

3. Allowing at least ¹/₄" for seam allowances on background *top* and *bottom* edges and matching raw edges on *side* edges, randomly position 2-3 **appliqués** on each background **(Fig. 2)**

Fig. 2

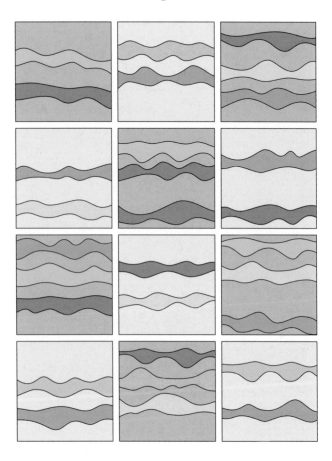

4. When satisfied with the placement, pin appliqués in place. Topstitch close to the faced curves of each appliqué to make **Block**. Make 12 Blocks.

Block (make 12)

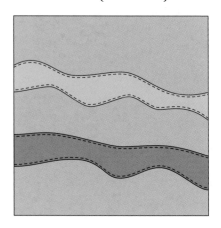

5. Keeping Blocks in the same order as your design wall, sew 3 Blocks together to make a **Row**. Make 4 Rows.
6. Sew Rows together to complete the **Quilt Top**.

COMPLETING THE QUILT

1. Follow **Quilting**, page 55, to mark, layer, and quilt as desired. The model is machine quilted with echo quilting and randomly placed flower motifs. The first row of echo quilting is about ¹/₂" from the edges of the appliqués then the additional rows are about 1" apart. The flowers are free-motion quilted.
2. If desired, follow **Adding A Hanging Sleeve**, page 59, to add a hanging sleeve.
3. Use **binding strips** and follow **Binding**, page 59, to make and attach **straight-grain binding**.

BATH MAT

SHOWN ON PAGE 37

MAKE BATH TIME EVEN MORE FUN WHEN YOU DECORATE YOUR BATHROOM WITH
THIS CUTE TERRY CLOTH MAT APPLIQUÉD WITH EVERYONE'S FAVORITE BATH TOY!

Finished Bath Mat Size: 30" x 20" (76 cm x 51 cm)

WHAT YOU WILL NEED
*Yardage is based on 43"/44" (109 cm/112 cm) fabric
with a usable width of 40".*
- $5/8$ yd (57 cm) of white terry cloth fabric
- $3/8$ yd (34 cm) of blue terry cloth fabric
- $5/8$ yd (57 cm) of yellow solid fabric (duck and binding)
- $3/8$ yd (34 cm) of facing fabric
- $3/4$ yd (69 cm) of backing fabric
- 34" x 24" (86 cm x 61 cm) rectangle of batting
- Tracing paper
- Removable fabric marking pen or pencil

CUTTING
*Cut all strips across the selvage to selvage width of the
fabric. All measurements include $1/4$" seam allowances.*
From white terry cloth fabric:
- Cut 1 **background** $29^1/2$" x $19^1/2$" wide.

From blue terry cloth fabric:
- Cut 1 **rectangle** $29^1/2$" x 12".

From yellow solid fabric:
- Cut 3 **binding strips** $2^1/2$" wide.
- Cut 1 **duck rectangle** 16" x 12".

From facing fabric:
- Cut 1 **facing rectangle** 16" x 12".

From backing fabric:
- Cut 1 **backing** 34" x 24".

Continued on page 36.

Bath Mat continued.

MAKING THE BATH MAT
Match right sides and raw edges and use a ¹/₄" seam allowance unless otherwise noted.

1. Trace **duck pattern**, pages 38-39, onto tracing paper; cut out.
2. Using duck pattern, **duck rectangle**, and **facing rectangle**, follow **Making Closed Appliqués**, page 11, to make **duck appliqué**.
3. Fold 1 long edge of blue terry cloth **rectangle** approximately 4" to the right side; pin (**Fig. 1**). Follow **Making Single Appliqués**, page 7, to make a faced curve along folded edge to make **water appliqué**.

Fig. 1

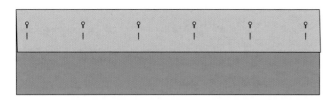

Water Appliqué

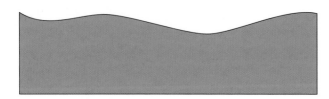

4. Matching bottom and side raw edges, position water appliqué on **background**. Tucking bottom edge of duck under faced curve of water, position duck appliqué on background (**Fig. 2**). Pin duck appliqué in place; remove water appliqué.

Fig. 2

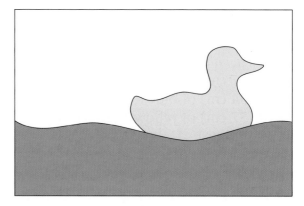

5. Topstitch through all layers along the faced curves of duck appliqué (**Fig. 3**).

Fig. 3

6. Reposition water; pin. Topstitch through all layers along the faced curve of the water appliqué to make **Bath Mat Top**.

Continued on page 38.

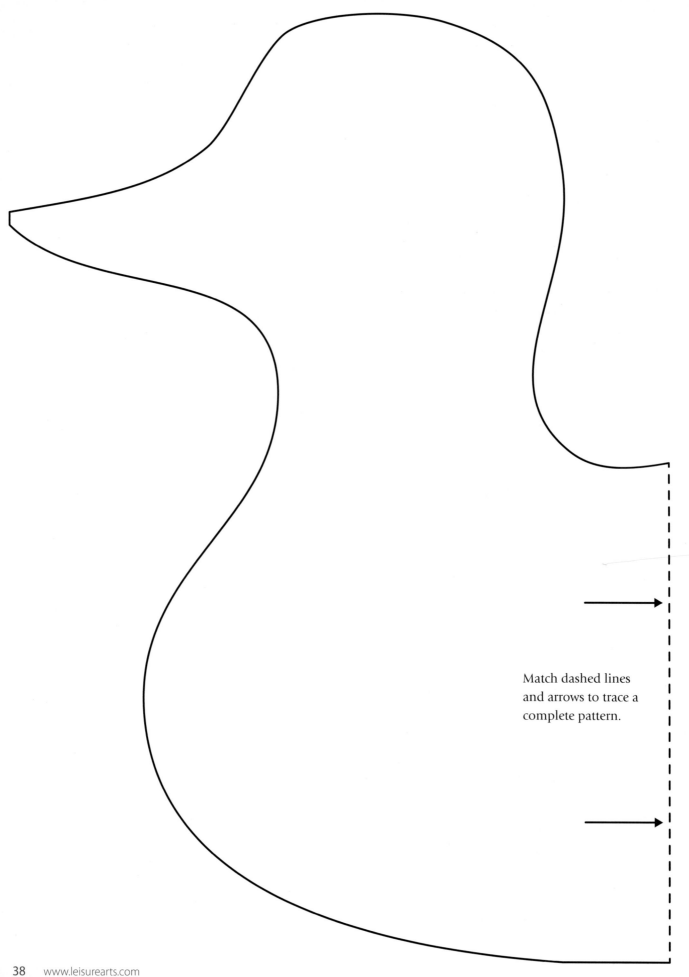

Match dashed lines
and arrows to trace a
complete pattern.

Bath Mat continued.

COMPLETING THE BATH MAT

1. Using **batting, backing**, and **bath mat top**, follow **Quilting**, page 55, to mark, layer, and quilt as desired. The model is machine outline quilted around the duck. The water and background have echo quilting, spaced 1" apart, following the curve of the water.

2. Use **binding strips** and follow **Binding**, page 59, to make and attach **straight-grain binding** to bath mat.

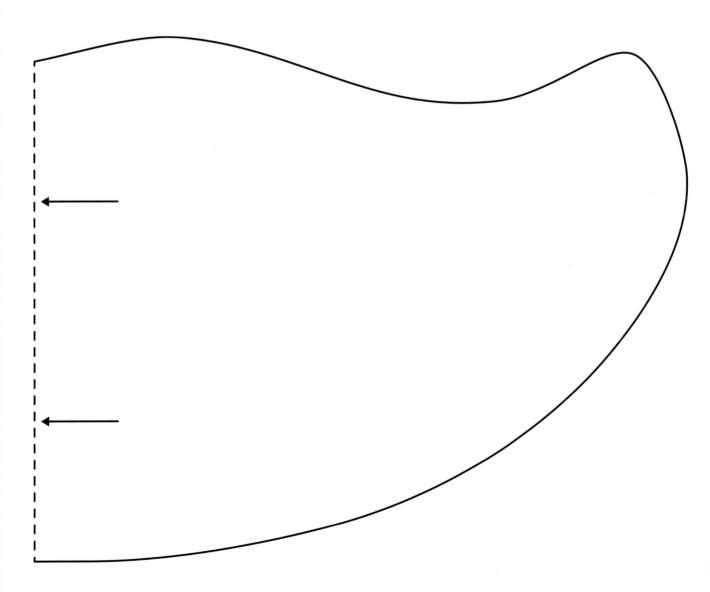

TABLE RUNNER
& PLACEMATS

This set of four placemats and a table runner makes a cheerful addition to any dining table. Because they are so quick and easy, you may want to make several sets in different colorways.

TABLE RUNNER
Finished Size: 13" x 48" (33 cm x 122 cm)

WHAT YOU WILL NEED
Yardage is based on 43"/44" (109 cm/112 cm) fabric with a usable width of 40".

- $1^{1}/_2$ yds (1.4 m) of grey/yellow print fabric (main fabric)
- $^{1}/_4$ yd (23 cm) of grey print fabric (small circles)
- $^{3}/_4$ yd (69 cm) of yellow solid fabric (medium circles)
- $^{3}/_4$ yd (69 cm) of facing fabric
- $1^{1}/_2$ yds (1.4 m) of backing fabric
- $^{3}/_8$ yd (34 cm) of binding fabric
- 17" x 52" (43 cm x 132 cm) rectangle of heat-resistant batting such as Insul-Bright® or Insul Fleece™
- Template plastic
- Black fine-point permanent felt-tip pen
- Removable fabric marking pen or pencil

CUTTING THE PIECES
Cut all strips across the selvage to selvage width of the fabric. All measurements include $^{1}/_4$" seam allowances.

From grey/yellow print fabric:
- Cut 1 *lengthwise* **table runner background** $12^{1}/_2$" x $47^{1}/_2$".

From grey print fabric:
- Cut 4 **small appliqué squares** 8" x 8".

From yellow solid fabric:
- Cut 4 **medium appliqué squares** 11" x 11".

From facing fabric:
- Cut 4 **facing squares** 11" x 11".

From backing fabric:
- Cut 1 *lengthwise* **table runner backing** 17" x 52".

From binding fabric:
- Cut 4 **binding strips** $2^{1}/_2$" wide.

MAKING THE TABLE RUNNER
*Match right sides and raw edges and use a $^{1}/_4$" seam allowance unless otherwise noted. Follow **Making And Using Templates**, page 54, to make templates from the small and medium circle patterns, page 52.*

1. Using the medium circle template, **medium appliqué squares** and **facing squares**, follow **Making Closed Appliqués**, page 11, to make 4 **medium circle appliqués**.

Medium Circle Appliqué (make 4)

2. Matching raw edges, fold 1 medium circle in half; press to crease. Open and cut along crease to make 2 **half-circle appliqués**.

Half-Circle Appliqué (make 2)

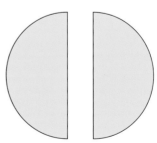

Continued on page 42.

Table Runner continued.

3. Using the small circle template, **small appliqué squares**, and facing fabric circles left over from the centers of medium circle appliqués, make 4 **small circle appliqués**.

Small Circle Appliqué (make 4)

4. Arrange 2 half circle, 3 medium circle, and 4 small circle appliqués on **table runner background**; pin.

Table Runner

COMPLETING THE TABLE RUNNER

The circles are stitched to the background while quilting the table runner.

1. Using **table runner batting, table runner backing**, and **table runner background**, follow **Quilting**, page 55, to mark, layer, and quilt as desired. The model is machine quilted. The circle appliqués are stitched through all layers, close to the edge of each appliqué. There is a flower quilted in the center of each appliqué. The background is quilted with an all-over leaf design.

2. Use **binding strips** and follow **Binding**, page 59, to make and attach **straight-grain binding** to Table Runner.

PLACEMATS
Finished Size: 13" x 18" (33 cm x 46 cm)

WHAT YOU WILL NEED
Yardage is based on 43"/44" (109 cm/112 cm) fabric with a usable width of 40". Fabric requirements are for 4 Placemats.

$^7/_8$ yd (80 cm) of grey/yellow print fabric (main fabric)*

$^1/_4$ yd (23 cm) of grey print fabric (small circles)

$^3/_4$ yd (69 cm) of yellow solid fabric (medium circles)

$^3/_4$ yd (69 cm) of facing fabric

$1^3/_8$ yds (1.3 m) of backing fabric*

$^5/_8$ yd (57 cm) of binding fabric

37" x 48" (94 cm x 122 cm) rectangle of heat-resistant batting such as Insul-Bright® or Insul Fleece™

Template plastic

Black fine-point permanent felt-tip pen

Removable fabric marking pen or pencil

* If you are making the placemats *and* table runner, purchase yardage for the table runner only. After cutting the table runner pieces, the placemat backgrounds and placemat backings can be cut from the remaining widths of the table runner fabric.

CUTTING THE PIECES

Cut all strips across the selvage to selvage width of the fabric. All measurements include $1/4$" seam allowances.

From grey/yellow print fabric:
- Cut 4 **placemat backgrounds** $12^1/_2$" x $17^1/_2$".

From grey print fabric:
- Cut 4 **small squares** 8" x 8".

From yellow solid fabric:
- Cut 4 **medium squares** 11" x 11".

From facing fabric:
- Cut 4 **medium squares** 11" x 11".

From backing fabric:
- Cut 4 **placemat backings** 17" x 22".

From binding fabric:
- Cut 7 **binding strips** $2^1/_2$" wide.

From batting:
- Cut 4 **placemat battings** 17" x 22".

MAKING THE PLACEMATS

*Match right sides and raw edges and use a $1/4$" seam allowance unless otherwise noted. Follow **Making And Using Templates**, page 54, to make templates from the small and medium circle patterns, page 52.*

1. Using the medium circle template, yellow **medium squares** and facing fabric **medium squares**, follow **Making Closed Appliqués**, page 10, to make 4 **medium circle appliqués**.

Medium Circle Appliqué (make 4)

2. Using the small circle template, grey **small squares**, and facing fabric circles left over from the centers of large circles, make 4 **small circle appliqués**.

Small Circle Appliqué (make 4)

3. Referring to **Placemat Diagram**, arrange 1 medium circle and 1 small circle appliqué on each **placemat background**; pin.

Placemat Diagram

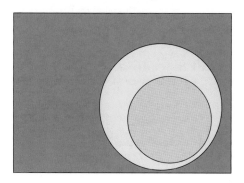

COMPLETING THE PLACEMATS

The circle appliqués are stitched to the backgrounds while quilting the placemats.

1. Using **placemat battings, placemat backings**, and **placemat backgrounds** follow **Quilting**, page 55, to mark, layer, and quilt each placemat as desired. The models are machine quilted. The appliqués are stitched through all layers, close to the edges of the appliqués. There is a flower quilted in the center of each small circle. The background is quilted with an all-over leaf design.

2. Use **binding strips** and follow **Binding**, page 59, to make and attach **straight-grain binding** to each placemat.

JAMBALAYA

THIS REFRESHING BLUE AND GREEN QUILT FEATURES SEVERAL TECHNIQUES INCLUDING MAKING PIECED INSERTS FROM SINGLE APPLIQUÉS, REVERSE APPLIQUÉ TO FRAME THE INSERTS, AND CLOSED APPLIQUÉ TO MAKE THE CIRCLES.

Finished Quilt Size: 46" x 46" (117 cm x 117 cm)
Finished Block Size: 15" x 15" (38 cm x 38 cm)

WHAT YOU WILL NEED

Yardage is based on 43"/44" (109 cm/112 cm) fabric with a usable width of 40".

- $2^3/_8$ yds (2.2 m) of cream print fabric (background squares)
- $3/_8$ yd (34 cm) *each* of 4 assorted blue and 4 assorted pink print fabrics (insert fabrics)
- $7/_8$ yd (80 cm) blue solid fabric (pieced blocks)
- $1^1/_8$ yds (1 m) green solid fabric (pieced blocks)
- $1^1/_4$ yds (1.1 m) of facing fabric
- 3 yds (2.7 m) of backing fabric
- $1/_2$ yd (46 cm) of binding fabric
- 54" x 54" (137 cm x 137 cm) square of batting
- Template plastic
- Black fine-point permanent felt-tip pen
- Removable fabric marking pen or pencil

CUTTING

Cut all strips across the selvage to selvage width of the fabric. All measurements include $1/_4$" seam allowances.

From cream print fabric:
- Cut 5 strips $15^1/_2$" wide. From these strips, cut 9 **background squares** $15^1/_2$" x $15^1/_2$".

From assorted blue and pink print fabrics:
- Cut 6 blue and 6 pink **strips** 6" wide.

From blue solid fabric:
- Cut 3 strips 9" wide. From these strips, cut 8 **rectangles** 9" x $12^1/_2$".

From green solid fabric:
- Cut 4 strips 9" wide. From these strips, cut 10 **rectangles** 9" x $12^1/_2$".

From facing fabric:
- Cut 3 strips $12^1/_2$" wide. From these strips, cut 9 **squares** $12^1/_2$" x $12^1/_2$".

From binding fabric:
- Cut 6 **binding strips** $2^1/_2$" wide.

Continued on page 46.

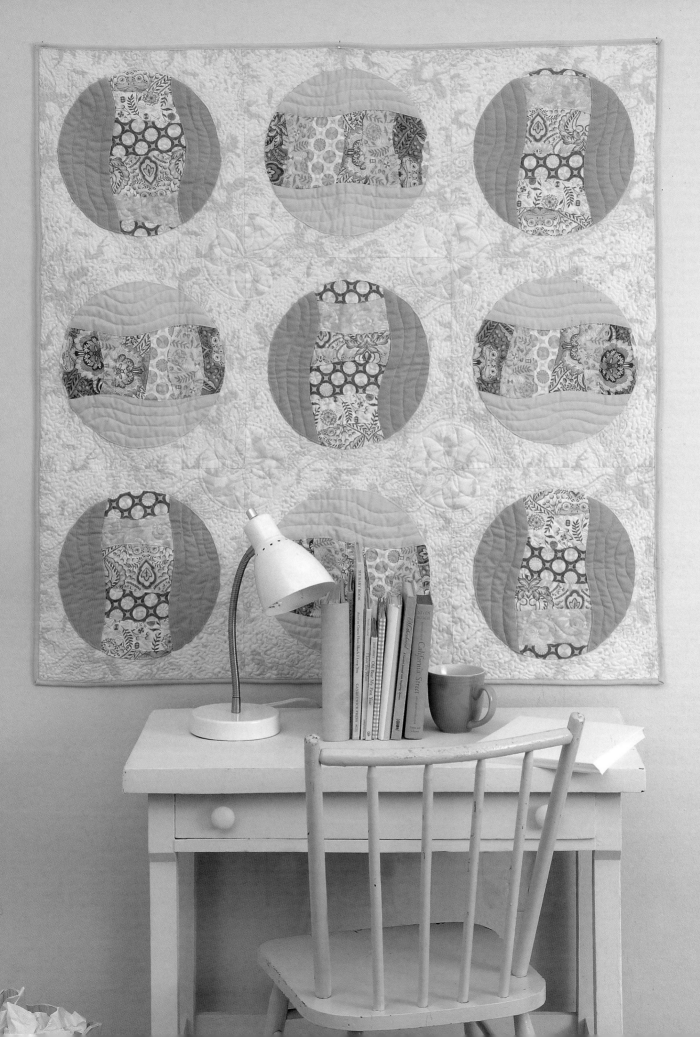

45

4

45

MAKING THE QUILT TOP

*Match right sides and raw edges and use a $^1/_4$" seam allowance unless otherwise noted. Follow **Making And Using Templates**, page 54, to make a template from the large circle pattern, page 52.*

Making The Strip Sets

1. Fold 1 long edge of 1 **strip** approximately 2" to the right side; pin (**Fig. 1**). Following **Making Single Appliqués**, page 7, make a shallow, gently rolling faced curve along folded edge to make **appliqué A**. Make 5 pink and 5 blue **appliqué A's**. Leave 1 blue and 1 pink strip unfaced.

Fig. 1

Appliqué A (make 5 pink and 5 blue)

2. For each strip set, select 1 **unfaced** and 5 **appliqué A's** from the same color group. Refer to **Gentle Curves**, page 18, Making The Strip Sets, Steps 2 -7, to make a **pieced insert** that measures 8" x 14$^1/_2$". Square insert to 8" x 12$^1/_2$". Make 5 blue and 4 pink pieced inserts.

Pieced Insert (make 5 blue and 4 pink)

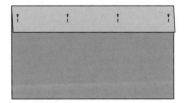

Making The Blocks

1. Fold 1 long edge of 1 blue or green **rectangle** approximately 2" to the right side; pin (**Fig. 2**). Following **Making Single Appliqués**, page 7, make a shallow, gently rolling faced curve along folded edge to make **appliqué B**. Make 9 pairs of appliqué B's.

Fig. 2

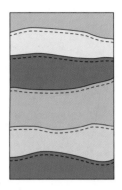

Appliqué B (make 9 pairs)

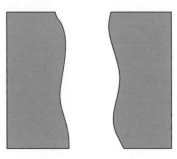

2. Position 1 pair of appliqué B's on 1 **pieced insert**. Adjust placement of appliqué B's until you are please with the look. You can allow any amount of pieced insert to show as long as your block is at *least* 12¹/₂" wide. Follow **Making Reverse Appliqués**, page 9, to make **reverse appliqué**.

3. Trim reverse appliqué to 12¹/₂" x 12¹/₂" to make **Pieced Block**. Make 9 Pieced Blocks.

Pieced Block (make 9)

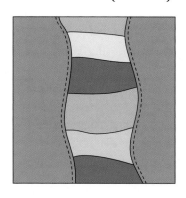

4. Using the large circle template, Pieced Blocks, and facing fabric **squares**, follow **Making Closed Appliqués**, page 11, to make 9 **circle appliqués**.

Circle Appliqué (make 9)

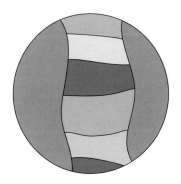

5. Arrange 1 circle appliqué on 1 **background square**; pin.

6. Stitching ¹/₈" from faced edges, sew circle to background square to make **Block**. Make 9 Blocks.

Block (make 9)

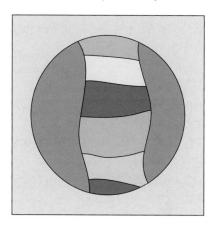

Assembling The Quilt Top

1. Sew 3 Blocks together to make a **Row**. Make 3 Rows.

2. Sew Rows together to make the **Quilt Top**.

COMPLETING THE QUILT

1. Follow **Quilting**, page 55, to mark, layer, and quilt as desired. The model is machine quilted with a flower motif at the intersections of the blocks. The remainder of the background is meander quilted. Each circle is quilted with swirls in the insert and echo quilting in the blue and green areas.

2. If desired, follow **Adding A Hanging Sleeve**, page 59, to make and attach a hanging sleeve.

3. Use **binding strips** and follow **Binding**, page 59, to make and attach **straight-grain binding**.

STACKED CIRCLES

This bright quilt is made from bold colorful print fabrics and pieces cut from a retired military uniform. Quilts featuring uniform pieces show support and help family members at home feel close to their deployed loved ones.

Finished Quilt Size: 61" x 61" (155 cm x 155 cm)
Finished Block Size: 15" x 15" (38 cm x 38 cm)

WHAT YOU WILL NEED

Yardage is based on 43"/44" (109 cm/112 cm) fabric with a usable width of 40".

- 1 military uniform (shirt and pants) *or*
  1³/₄ yds (1.6 m) of print fabric
- ¹/₂ yd (46 cm) *each* of 16 assorted
  print fabrics
- 2¹/₂ yds (2.3 m) of neutral color
  facing fabric
- 3⁷/₈ yds (3.5 m) of backing fabric
- ⁵/₈ yd (57 cm) of binding fabric
- 69" x 69" (175 cm x 175 cm) square
  of batting
- Template plastic
- Black fine-point permanent felt-tip pen
- Removable fabric marking pen or pencil

CUTTING

Cut all strips across the selvage to selvage width of the fabric. All measurements include ¹/₄" seam allowances.

From military uniform or print fabric:
- Cut 8 **large appliqué squares** 13" x 13".*
- Cut 8 **small appliqué squares** 9" x 9".

From assorted print fabrics:
- Cut a *total* of 16 **background squares**
  15¹/₂" x 15¹/₂".
- Cut a *total* of 8 **large appliqué squares**
  13" x 13".
- Cut a *total* of 8 **small appliqué squares**
  9" x 9".

From facing fabric:
- Cut 6 strips 13" wide. From these strips,
  cut 16 **facing squares** 13" x 13".

From binding fabric:
- Cut 7 **binding strips** 2¹/₂" wide.

*Before cutting, remove any buttons, zippers, and insignia from the uniform pieces. Do not remove pockets. Squares should be cut to include pieces of pockets and seams.

Continued on page 50.

MAKING THE QUILT TOP

*Match right sides and raw edges and use a ¹/₄" seam allowance unless otherwise noted. Follow **Making And Using Templates**, page 54, to make templates from small and large circle patterns, page 52.*

1. Using the large circle template, uniform fabric and print fabric **large appliqué squares,** and **facing squares,** follow **Making Closed Appliqués,** page 10, to make 16 **large circle appliqués**.

    Large Circle Appliqué (make 16)

2. Using the small circle template, uniform fabric and print fabric **small appliqué squares,** and facing fabric circles left over from the centers of large circles, make 16 **small circle appliqués**.

    Small Circle Appliqué (make 16)

3. Randomly arrange 1 large and 1 small circle appliqué on 1 **background square**; pin.
4. Stitching ¹/₈" from faced edges, sew large and small circles to background square to make **Block**. Make 16 Blocks.

    Block (make 16)

    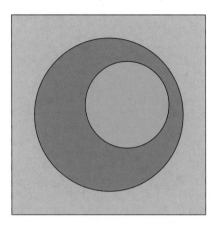

5. Sew 4 Blocks together to make a **Row**. Make 4 Rows.
6. Sew Rows together to make the **Quilt Top**.

COMPLETING THE QUILT

1. Follow **Quilting**, page 55, to mark, layer, and quilt as desired. The model is machine quilted with all-over meandering quilting.
2. If desired, follow **Adding A Hanging Sleeve**, page 59, to make and attach a hanging sleeve.
3. Use **binding strips** and follow **Binding**, page 59, to make and attach **straight-grain binding**.

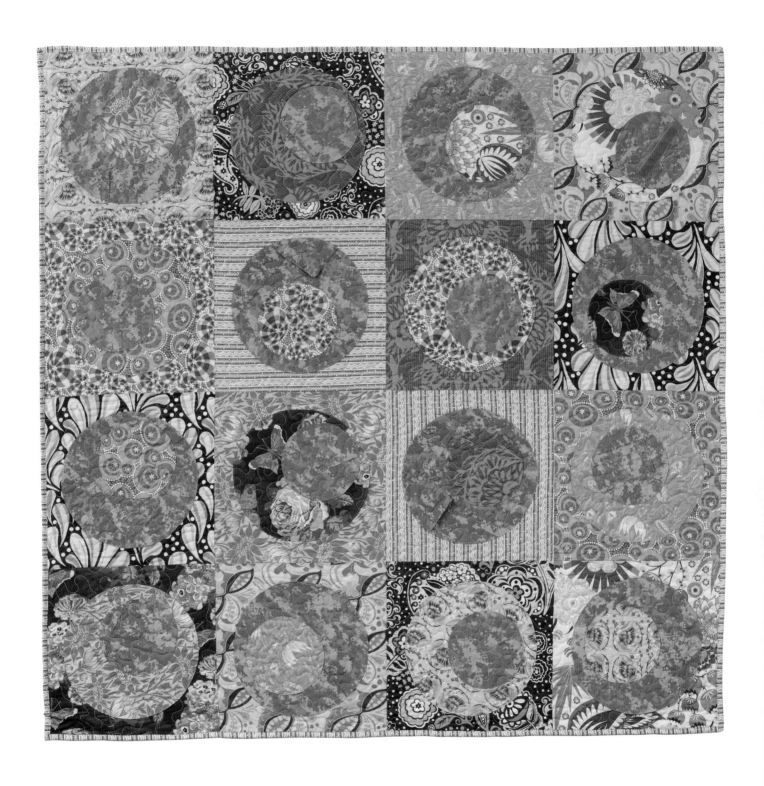

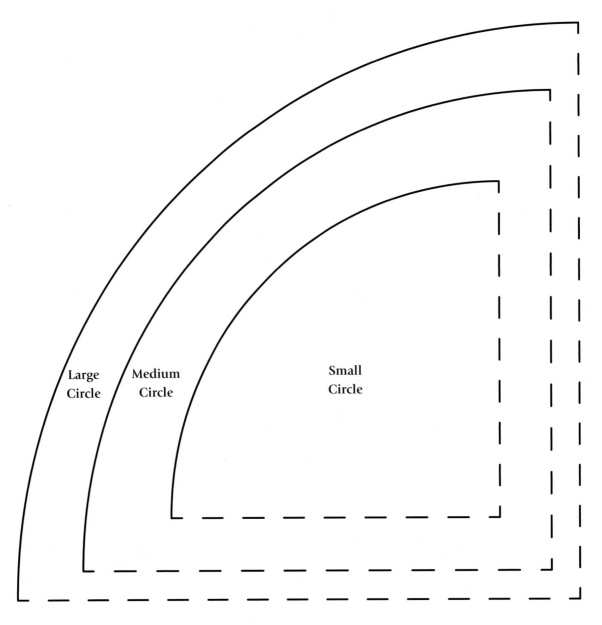

Large
Circle

Medium
Circle

Small
Circle

To trace a complete circle pattern, trace quarter pattern onto template plastic. Rotate plastic $^1/_4$ turn and trace pattern again. Continue rotating and tracing until a complete circle is traced.

GENERAL INSTRUCTIONS

We recommend that all fabric be washed, dried, and pressed before cutting. If fabrics are not pre-washed, washing the finished quilt will cause shrinkage and give it a more "antiqued" look and feel. Bright and dark colors, which may run, should always be washed before cutting. After washing and drying fabric, fold lengthwise with wrong sides together and matching selvages.

Before cutting, prepare fabrics with a steam iron set on cotton and starch or sizing. The starch or sizing will give the fabric a crisp finish. This will make cutting more accurate and may make piecing easier.

ROTARY CUTTING

- Place fabric on work surface with fold closest to you.

- Cut all strips from the selvage-to-selvage width of the fabric unless otherwise indicated in project instructions.

- Square left edge of fabric using rotary cutter and rulers (**Figs. 1-2**).

Fig. 1

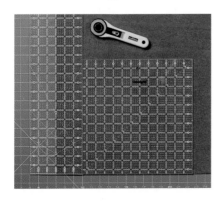

Fig. 2

- To cut each strip required for a project, place ruler over cut edge of fabric, aligning desired marking on ruler with cut edge; make cut (**Fig. 3**).

Fig. 3

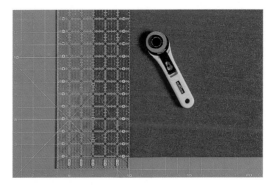

- When cutting several strips from a single piece of fabric, it is important to make sure that cuts remain at a perfect right angle to the fold; square fabric as needed.

MAKING AND USING TEMPLATES

1. To make a template from a drawn curve, use a permanent fine-point pen to carefully trace the curve onto template plastic. Cut out template along inner edge of drawn line.
2. To use a template, place the template face up on the wrong side of the fabric. Use a removable fabric-marking pen or pencil to draw around template onto the fabric.

PIECING

Precise cutting, followed by accurate piecing, will ensure that all pieces of quilt top fit together well.

- Set sewing machine stitch length for approximately 11 stitches per inch.

- Use neutral-colored general-purpose sewing thread (not quilting thread) in the needle and in the bobbin.

- An accurate $1/4$" seam allowance is *essential*. Presser feet that are $1/4$" wide are available for most sewing machines.

- When piecing, always place pieces right sides together and match raw edges; pin if necessary.

- Chain piecing saves time and will usually result in more accurate piecing.

- Trim away points of seam allowances that extend beyond edges of sewn pieces.

Sewing Across Seam Intersections

When sewing across the intersection of two seams, place pieces right sides together and match seams exactly, making sure seam allowances are pressed in opposite directions (**Fig. 4**).

Fig. 4

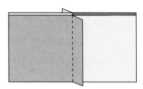

PRESSING

- Use a steam iron set on "Cotton" for all pressing.

- Press after sewing each seam.

- Seam allowances are almost always pressed to one side, usually toward the darker fabric. However, to reduce bulk it may occasionally be necessary to press seam allowances toward the lighter fabric or even to press them open.

- To prevent dark fabric seam allowance from showing through light fabric, trim darker seam allowance slightly narrower than lighter seam allowance.

- To press long seams, such as those in long strip sets, without curving or other distortion, lay strips across width of the ironing board.

QUILTING

*Quilting holds the three layers (top, batting, and backing) of the quilt together. Because marking, layering, and quilting are interrelated and may be done in different orders depending on circumstances, please read entire **Quilting** section, pages 55-58, before beginning project.*

TYPES OF QUILTING DESIGNS

In the Ditch Quilting

Quilting along seamlines or along edges of appliquéd pieces is called "in the ditch" quilting. This type of quilting should be done on side **opposite** seam allowance and does not have to be marked.

Outline Quilting

Quilting a consistent distance, usually $1/4$", from seam or appliqué is called "outline" quilting. Outline quilting may be marked, or $1/4$" masking tape may be placed along seamlines for quilting guide. (Do not leave tape on quilt longer than necessary, since it may leave an adhesive residue.)

Motif Quilting

Quilting a design, such as a feathered wreath, is called "motif" quilting. This type of quilting should be marked before basting quilt layers together.

Echo Quilting

Quilting that follows the outline of an appliquéd or pieced design with two or more parallel lines is called "echo" quilting. This type of quilting does not need to be marked.

Meandering Quilting

Quilting in random curved lines and swirls is called "meandering" quilting. Quilting lines should not cross or touch each other. This type of quilting does not need to be marked.

MARKING QUILTING LINES

Quilting lines may be marked using removable fabric marking pencils, chalk markers, or water- or air-soluble pens.

Simple quilting designs may be marked with chalk or chalk pencil after basting. A small area may be marked, then quilted, before moving to next area to be marked. Intricate designs should be marked before basting using a more durable marker.

Caution: Pressing may permanently set some marks. **Test** different markers **on scrap fabric** to find one that marks clearly and can be thoroughly removed.

A wide variety of pre-cut quilting stencils, as well as entire books of quilting patterns, are available. Using a stencil makes it easier to mark intricate or repetitive designs.

To make a stencil from a pattern, center template plastic over pattern and use a permanent marker to trace pattern onto plastic. Use a craft knife with single or double blade to cut channels along traced lines (**Fig. 5**).

Fig. 5

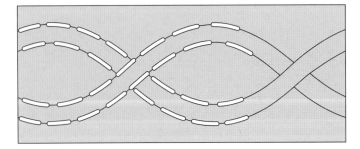

PREPARING THE BACKING

To allow for the slight shifting of the quilt top during quilting, the backing should be approximately 4" larger on all sides than the quilt top for large quilts and 2" larger on all sides for small quilts. Yardage requirements listed for quilt backings are calculated for 43"/44"w fabric. Using 90"w or 108"w fabric for the backing of a bed-sized quilt may eliminate piecing. To piece a backing using 43"/44"w fabric, use the following instructions.

1. Measure length and width of quilt top; add 8" to each measurement.

2. If determined width is 79" or less, cut backing fabric into two lengths slightly longer than determined *length* measurement. Trim selvages. Place lengths with right sides facing and sew long edges together, forming a tube (**Fig. 6**). Match seams and press along one fold (**Fig. 7**). Cut along pressed fold to form single piece (**Fig. 8**).

Fig. 6 **Fig. 7**

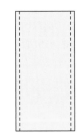 

Fig. 8

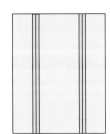

3. If determined width is more than 79", it may require less fabric yardage if the backing is pieced horizontally. Divide determined *length* measurement by 40" to determine how many widths will be needed. Cut required number of widths the determined *width* measurement. Trim selvages. Sew long edges together to form single piece.

4. Trim backing to size determined in Step 1; press seam allowances open.

CHOOSING THE BATTING

The appropriate batting will make quilting easier. For fine hand quilting, choose low-loft batting. All cotton or cotton/polyester blend battings work well for machine quilting because the cotton helps "grip" quilt layers. If quilt is to be tied, a high-loft batting, sometimes called extra-loft or fat batting, may be used to make quilt "fluffy."

Types of batting include cotton, polyester, wool, cotton/polyester blend, cotton/wool blend, and silk.

When selecting batting, refer to package labels for characteristics and care instructions. Cut batting same size as prepared backing.

ASSEMBLING THE QUILT

1. Examine the wrong side of the quilt top closely; trim any seam allowances and clip any threads that may show through front of the quilt. Press quilt top, being careful not to "set" any marked quilting lines.

2. Place backing *wrong* side up on a flat surface. Use masking tape to tape edges of backing to surface. Place batting on top of backing fabric. Smooth batting gently, being careful not to stretch or tear. Center quilt top *right* side up on batting.

3. Use 1" rustproof safety pins to "pin-baste" all layers together, spacing pins approximately 4" apart. Begin at center and work toward outer edges to secure all layers. If possible, place pins away from areas that will be quilted, although pins may be removed as needed when quilting.

MACHINE QUILTING METHODS

Use general-purpose thread in bobbin. Do not use quilting thread. Thread the machine needle with general-purpose thread or transparent monofilament thread to make quilting blend with quilt top fabrics. Use decorative thread, such as a metallic or contrasting-color general-purpose thread, to make quilting lines stand out more.

Straight-Line Quilting

The term "straight-line" is somewhat deceptive, since curves (especially gentle ones) as well as straight lines can be stitched with this technique.

1. Set stitch length for six to ten stitches per inch and attach a walking foot to sewing machine.
2. Determine which section of the quilt will have the longest continuous quilting line, oftentimes the area from the center top to center bottom. Roll up and secure each edge of quilt to help reduce the bulk, keeping fabrics smooth. Smaller projects may not need to be rolled.
3. Begin stitching on longest quilting line, using very short stitches for the first $1/4$" to "lock" quilting. Stitch across project, using one hand on each side of walking foot to slightly spread fabric and to guide fabric through machine. Lock stitches at end of quilting line.
4. Continue machine quilting, stitching longer quilting lines first to stabilize quilt before moving on to other areas.

Free-Motion Quilting

Free-motion quilting may be free form or may follow a marked pattern.

1. Attach a darning foot to the sewing machine and lower or cover feed dogs.
2. Position the quilt under the darning foot; lower foot. Holding top thread, take a stitch and pull bobbin thread to top of quilt. To "lock" beginning of quilting line, hold top and bobbin threads while making three to five stitches in place.
3. Use one hand on each side of darning foot to slightly spread fabric and to move fabric through the machine. Even stitch length is achieved by using smooth, flowing hand motion and steady machine speed. Slow machine speed and fast hand movement will create long stitches. Fast machine speed and slow hand movement will create short stitches. Move quilt sideways, back and forth, in a circular motion, or in a random motion to create desired designs; do not rotate quilt. Lock stitches at end of each quilting line.

ADDING A HANGING SLEEVE

Attaching a hanging sleeve to back of wall hanging or quilt before the binding is added allows project to be displayed on wall.

1. Measure width of quilt top edge and subtract 1". Cut piece of fabric 7"w by determined measurement.
2. Press short edges of fabric piece $1/4$" to wrong side; press edges $1/4$" to wrong side again and machine stitch in place.
3. Matching wrong sides, fold piece in half lengthwise to form tube.
4. Before sewing binding to quilt top, match raw edges and pin hanging sleeve to center top edge on back of quilt; stitch in place.
5. Bind quilt, treating hanging sleeve as part of backing.
6. Blindstitch bottom of hanging sleeve to backing, taking care not to stitch through to front of quilt.

BLIND STITCH

Come up at 1, go down at 2, and come up at 3 (**Fig. 9**). Length of stitches may be varied as desired.

Fig. 9

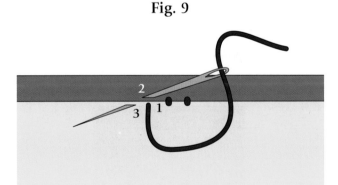

BINDING

Binding encloses the raw edges of quilt. Follow the instructions below to make and attach binding.

MAKING STRAIGHT-GRAIN BINDING

1. To piece binding strips, use the diagonal seams method (**Fig. 10**). Press seam allowances open.

Fig. 10

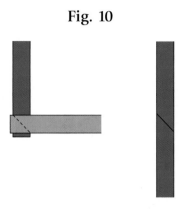

2. Matching wrong sides and raw edges, press strip(s) in half lengthwise to complete the binding.

ATTACHING BINDING

For a quick and easy finish when attaching straight-grain binding, sew the binding to the back of the quilt and machine straight stitch it in place on the front, eliminating all hand stitching.

1. Using a narrow zigzag, stitch around quilt close to the raw edges (**Fig. 11**). Trim backing and batting even with edges of quilt top.

Fig. 11

2. Beginning with one end near center on bottom edge of quilt, lay binding around quilt to make sure that seams in binding will not end up at a corner. Adjust placement if necessary. Matching raw edges of binding to raw edge of quilt top, pin binding to backing side of quilt along one edge.

3. When you reach first corner, mark ¹/₄" from corner of quilt top (**Fig. 12**).

Fig. 12

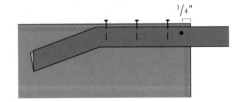

4. Beginning approximately 10" from end of binding and using a ¹/₄" seam allowance, sew binding to quilt, backstitching at beginning of stitching and at mark (**Fig. 13**). Lift needle out of fabric and clip thread.

Fig. 13

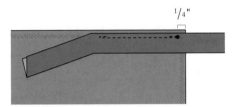

5. Fold binding as shown in **Figs. 14–15** and pin binding to adjacent side, matching raw edges. When you've reached the next corner, mark ¹/₄" from edge of quilt top.

Fig. 14

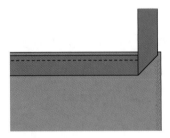

Fig. 15

6. Backstitching at edge of quilt top, sew pinned binding to quilt (**Fig. 16**); backstitch at the next mark. Lift needle out of fabric and clip thread.

Fig. 16

7. Continue sewing binding to quilt, stopping approximately 10" from starting point (**Fig. 17**).

Fig. 17

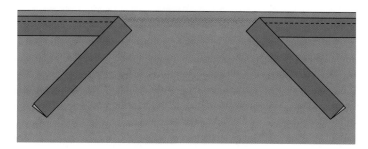

8. Bring beginning and end of binding to center of opening and fold each end back, leaving a $^1/_4$" space between folds (**Fig. 18**). Finger press folds.

Fig. 18

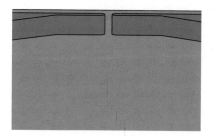

9. Unfold ends of binding and draw a line across wrong side in finger-pressed crease. Draw a line through the lengthwise pressed fold of binding at the same spot to create a cross mark. With edge of ruler at cross mark, line up 45° angle marking on ruler with one long side of binding. Draw a diagonal line from edge to edge. Repeat on remaining end, making sure that the two diagonal lines are angled the same way (**Fig. 19**).

Fig. 19

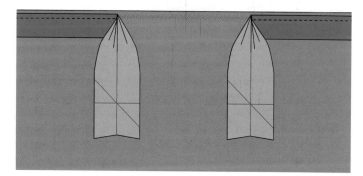

10. Matching right sides and diagonal lines, pin binding ends together at right angles (**Fig. 20**).

Fig. 20

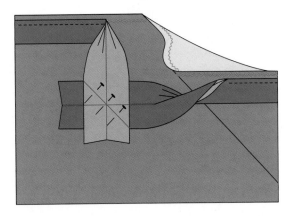

11. Machine stitch along diagonal line (**Fig. 21**), removing pins as you stitch.

Fig. 21

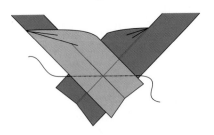

12. Lay binding against quilt to double check that it is correct length.
13. Trim binding ends, leaving $^1/_4$" seam allowance; press seam open. Stitch binding to quilt.

14. On one edge of quilt, fold binding over to quilt front and pin pressed edge in place, covering stitching line (**Fig. 22**). On adjacent side, fold binding over, forming a mitered corner (**Fig. 23**). Repeat to pin remainder of binding in place.

Fig. 22

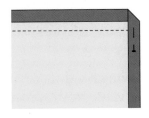

Fig. 23

15. Straight Stitch folded edge of the binding to the quilt front.

SIGNING AND DATING YOUR QUILT

A completed quilt is a work of art and should be signed and dated. There are many different ways to do this and numerous books on the subject. The label should reflect the style of the quilt, the occasion or person for which it was made, and the quilter's own particular talents. Following are suggestions for recording the history of the quilt or adding a sentiment for future generations.

- Embroider quilter's name, date, and any additional information on the quilt top or backing. Matching floss, such as cream floss on a white border, will leave a subtle record. Bright or contrasting floss will make the information stand out.

- Make label from muslin and use a permanent marker to write information. Use different colored permanent markers to make label more decorative. Stitch label to back of quilt.

- Use photo-transfer paper to add an image to a white or cream fabric label. Stitch label to back of quilt.

- Piece an extra block from the quilt top pattern to use as a label. Add information with permanent fabric pen. Appliqué block to back of quilt.

- Write message on appliquéd design from quilt top. Attach appliqué to back of the quilt.

CARING FOR YOUR QUILT

- Wash your finished quilt in cold water on the gentle cycle with mild soap. Soaps such as Orvus® Paste or Charlie's Soap®, which have no softeners, fragrances, whiteners, or other additives are safest. Rinse twice in cold water.

- Use a dye magnet such as Shout® Color Catcher® each time quilt is washed to absorb any dyes that bled. When washing a quilt for the first time, you may choose to use two dye magnets for extra caution.

- Dry quilt on low heat/air fluff in 15 minute increments until dry.

Metric Conversion Chart

Inches x 2.54 = centimeters (cm)	Yards x .9144 = meters (m)
Inches x 25.4 = millimeters (mm)	Yards x 91.44 = centimeters (cm)
Inches x .0254 = meters (m)	Centimeters x .3937 = inches (")
	Meters x 1.0936 = yards (yd)

Standard Equivalents

1/8"	3.2 mm	0.32 cm	1/8 yard	11.43 cm	0.11 m
1/4"	6.35 mm	0.635 cm	1/4 yard	22.86 cm	0.23 m
3/8"	9.5 mm	0.95 cm	3/8 yard	34.29 cm	0.34 m
1/2"	12.7 mm	1.27 cm	1/2 yard	45.72 cm	0.46 m
5/8"	15.9 mm	1.59 cm	5/8 yard	57.15 cm	0.57 m
3/4"	19.1 mm	1.91 cm	3/4 yard	68.58 cm	0.69 m
7/8"	22.2 mm	2.22 cm	7/8 yard	80 cm	0.8 m
1"	25.4 mm	2.54 cm	1 yard	91.44 cm	0.91 m

SPECIAL THANKS TO:

Free Spirit Fabrics, Michael Miller Fabrics. Riley Blake Fabrics,
Robert Kaufman Fabrics, Art Gallery Fabrics, and Fairfield Batting for
providing the fabrics and batting used to make the projects in this book.

Pattern testers - Karen Morello; Corinne Goeke; Beth Helfter; Chris Clark; and Melissa Stramel.

Colleen Eskridge, for the beautiful long arm quilting of the models.